THE PILGRIMS' FIRST THANKSGIVING

BY JESSICA GUNDERSON
ILLUSTRATED BY DEB LUCKE

PICTURE WINDOW BOOKS
a capstone imprint

Shots rang out through the quiet autumn air. A Native-American man named Massasoit stopped and listened. Massasoit was a Wampanoag leader.

The gunshots worried him. Was trouble lurking nearby? Were the colonists in danger? Quickly, Massasoit and 90 men set off into the woods. They headed toward the village of Plymouth.

4

The colonists of Plymouth also heard the gunshots. But the sound made them smile. Governor Bradford had sent four men into the forest to shoot wild birds. The gunshots meant the hunting party had found dinner. It was early fall, 1621. The colonists were celebrating a good harvest.

Nearly one year earlier, in 1620, more than 100 colonists had arrived in America. Many were Separatists, later called Pilgrims, who were seeking religious freedom.

The first year in Plymouth had been difficult. For the first few months, the Pilgrims lived in fear of the Native Americans they'd seen. And the food the Pilgrims had brought on their ship, the *Mayflower*, had run out quickly. Over the winter, nearly half of the Pilgrims died of starvation and disease.

One day in March 1621, a Native American man named Samoset walked into Plymouth. He said, "Welcome, Englishmen!" Samoset had learned English from traders who had come from Europe. It was the first time the Pilgrims were able to speak with a Native American.

Days later, Samoset brought Massasoit and an interpreter named Tisquantum (Squanto) to meet the Pilgrims. Massasoit and John Carver, Plymouth's first governor, signed a treaty. The treaty said that the Pilgrims and the Wampanoag would live in peace and help each other.

9

Tisquantum stayed with the Pilgrims. He showed them the best places to hunt and fish. He showed them how to plant corn, a grain important to Native Americans.

He planted the corn seeds in a mound and buried small fish with the seeds. This practice made the soil better for growing crops.

By autumn, the corn had grown tall. Other crops, such as squash and barley, were plentiful too. The Pilgrims caught large amounts of cod and shellfish. Winter was coming, but the Pilgrims weren't afraid this year. They knew they had enough food to last. They decided to celebrate the good harvest with a feast.

For three days, the Pilgrims and
the Wampanoag celebrated.

They ate deer meat and wild birds, fish and shellfish. They ate vegetables, pumpkin, corn cakes, and wild berries.

The children spent much of their time helping prepare the meals. They stirred the pots of bubbling stew over open fires. They ground corn and fetched water. But it wasn't all work! The children may have played running and jumping games, such as leap frog or hide-and-seek.

The adults enjoyed themselves too. The Wampanoag may have shown the Pilgrims some of their traditional dances. The Pilgrim men showed off their marching and shooting skills. Many of the Pilgrims may have also spent time praying.

19

After three days, Massasoit and the other Wampanoag bid the Pilgrims farewell. Winter would soon creep in. The Pilgrims knew there would be more work to do. But for now, everyone was full and happy.

Timeline of Key Dates

September 6, 1620
The *Mayflower* sets sail from Plymouth, England.

November 9, 1620
Land is sighted.

November 11, 1620
The *Mayflower* anchors in Cape Cod.

December 7, 1620
Pilgrim explorers encounter Native Americans. Shots are fired, but no one is injured.

December 20, 1620
The Pilgrims settle in Patuxet and rename it Plymouth. The Wampanoag had lived there until a few years before, when sickness destroyed most of the village.

March 16, 1621
An Abenaki Native American from Maine named Samoset walks into the village. He welcomes the settlers in English. He had learned to speak it from traders he'd met.

March 22, 1621
The Pilgrims sign a peace treaty with Massasoit, a leader of the Wampanoag people. The Wampanoag had lived in the area for thousands of years.

Late September/ Early October 1621
The Pilgrims and the Wampanoag gather for a three-day celebration in Plymouth.

Myth Busted

During the 1621 celebration, the colonists and the Wampanoag did not sit around a table to eat. There were not enough chairs for everyone. Instead, many people sat on benches or stools. Some sat on the ground or stood. They did not have forks. They ate with spoons, knives, and their fingers.

The 1621 Thanksgiving was not the first Thanksgiving in North America. The Native Americans often celebrated harvests. The Wampanoag celebrated the strawberry harvest in the spring and the green corn harvest in the summer. Earlier European settlers, such as those in Florida, Virginia, and Texas, held days of thanks for their blessings as well.

While the colonists did eat wild birds at the harvest feast, they may not have eaten turkey. They did not have potatoes. And they didn't have sugar to make cranberry sauce or pumpkin pie.

The Pilgrims did not always wear black clothing with white collars and wide buckles. Most of their clothing was colorful, made from natural dyes. If the Pilgrims had any black clothing, they wore it only for very special days. Black cloth was expensive.

Glossary

colonist—a person who leaves his or her country and settles in another land; when a group of colonists join together, they form a colony

harvest—the gathering of crops that are ripe

interpreter—a person who changes one language into another so people can understand each other

Pilgrim—one of the people who came to America in 1620 for religious freedom and set up Plymouth Colony; a pilgrim is also someone who goes on a religious journey

Separatist—a member of a religious group that split from the Church of England in the 1600s

starvation—dying from hunger

treaty—a written agreement between countries or groups of people

Read More

Englar, Mary. *The Pilgrims and the First Thanksgiving*. Graphic History. Mankato, Minn.: Capstone Press, 2007.

Shore, Diane. *This Is the Feast*. New York: HarperCollins Publishers, 2008.

Waters, Kate. *Giving Thanks: The 1621 Harvest Feast*. New York: Scholastic Press, 2001.

Internet Sites

FactHound offers a safe, fun way to find Internet sites related to this book. All of the sites on FactHound have been researched by our staff.

Here's all you do:

Visit *www.facthound.com*

Type in this code: 9781404862852

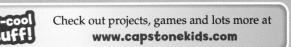

Super-cool stuff!

Check out projects, games and lots more at
www.capstonekids.com

Look for all the books in the Thanksgiving series:

Life on the Mayflower

The Pilgrims' First Thanksgiving

Thanksgiving Crafts

Thanksgiving Recipes

Thanksgiving Then and Now

Index

Special thanks to our advisers for their expertise:

Plimoth Plantation
Plymouth, Massachusetts

Terry Flaherty, PhD, Professor of English
Minnesota State University, Mankato

Editor: Jill Kalz
Designer: Alison Thiele
Art Director: Nathan Gassman
Production Specialist: Sarah Bennett
The illustrations in this book were created with gouache.

Picture Window Books
1710 Roe Crest Drive
North Mankato, MN 56003
877-845-8392
www.capstonepub.com

Library of Congress Cataloging-in-Publication Data
Gunderson, Jessica.
 The pilgrims' first Thanksgiving / by Jessica Gunderson ; illustrated by Deb Lucke.
    p. cm. — (Thanksgiving)
 Includes index.
 ISBN 978-1-4048-6285-2 (library binding)
 ISBN 978-1-4048-6720-8 (paperback)
 1. Thanksgiving Day—Juvenile literature. 2. Pilgrims (New Plymouth Colony)—Juvenile literature. 3. Massachusetts—History—New Plymouth, 1620–1691—Juvenile literature. I. Lucke, Deb, ill. II. Title.
 F7.G86 2011
 973.2'2—dc22   2010033767

Printed in the United States of America in North Mankato, Minnesota.
032014   008072R